For Stephanie, the answer to my most
fervent prayers, even those I dared not utter
aloud for fear of asking too much ... my
partner in healing, life and love.

LOOPS: The Secret Saboteurs of Intimacy and How to Get Rid of Them Forever

by Seth D. Eisenberg

Illustrated by Vasja Koman

Published by The PAIRS Foundation, Inc.

The PAIRS Foundation, Inc.
200 S. Park Road, Suite 455
Hollywood, FL 33021 USA
(877) PAIRS-4U - (877) 724-7748
Email: info@pairs.com
Online at www.pairs.com

ISBN-10: 0985427841.
ISBN-13: 978-0-9854278-4-9.

Printed by CreateSpace, An Amazon.com Company.
Available from Amazon.com and other online stores.

Manufactured in the United States of America.

A warrior and his beloved discover new depths of intimacy in PAIRS class.

THE LESSON OF LOOPS

Falling in love is the easy part. Timing. Luck. Patience. Persistence. At some moment in our lives, perhaps more than once, powerful forces of nature will deliver us face-to-face with a person we promise to love, honor and cherish for the rest of our lives.

Thirty years experience with thousands of couples in all stages of relationship - including many at the point of separation or divorce and others preparing to join their lives - offers ample evidence those vows are regularly exchanged with the most earnest intentions of heart, mind and soul.

Yet within years, sometimes less, the best of intentions too often become distant memories, broken promises, and painful surrenders that can scar lifetimes and generations.

What happens to love is profoundly connected to how couples navigate the "loops" that are unique to our closest relationships.

The lesson of loops is that the exit ramps from distance, disappointment and distress were never far away. Learning to identify and use those ramps offers the opportunity for deeper experiences of love, intimacy and happiness.

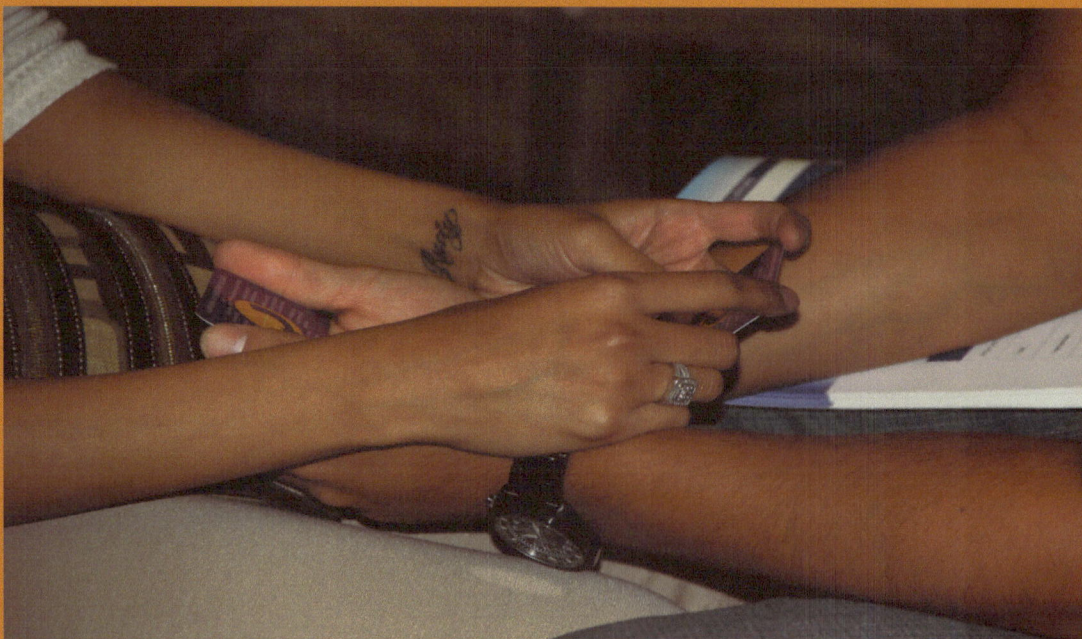

Couple finds deeper understanding, acceptance and love through confiding an emotional allergy.

EMOTIONAL ALLERGIES

Emotional experiences are stored in our long-term memory. Regardless of the passage of time, we remember what we feel. Painful or traumatic experiences are stored in a special way that can become "emotional allergies." Scientists are exploring how traumatic events of our parents, and potentially other ancestors, may also be imprinted in our DNA.

We are not always aware of our emotional allergies beyond knowing that some experiences and interactions cause intense, upsetting feelings.

Like physical allergies, emotional allergies are unique to each of us. Even twins can experience the same event and have significantly different responses. Events in the present can bring back painful feelings we had when we were hurt or frightened in the past. When something happens that reminds us of the past, we can get emotionally flooded, hijacked and feel overwhelmed. When we become flooded with painful feelings such as anger, sadness, fear, regret, guilt, or shame, we may not understand why we are so upset.

Loops begin with a reaction towards a significant other fueled by the intensity of an emotional allergy. It's that intensity that signals an emotional allergy has been triggered, offering the opportunity to choose to become reactive or risk being vulnerable.

That single decision can impact generations.

HOW TO USE THIS BOOK

Loops explores 12 of the most common emotional allergy infinity loops that cause relationship distress. The illustrated loops identify hidden assumptions and expectations, known as "love knots," that marriage and family therapist Lori Heyman Gordon, the founder of PAIRS, discusses more fully in her books, "If You Really Loved Me ..." and "Love Knots."

As you read the illustrated scenarios, consider which are familiar to you. When you find one that is, whether it seems identical or similar, use the Emotional Allergy Talking Tips (below) to confide about the allergy with a loved one whose role is simply to listen with empathy and repeat back your words so you know you're heard and understood. If you aren't able to do this with a partner, try the online version at apps.pairs.com.

Remember, emotional allergies are signaled by intensity. That's very different than experiences we don't enjoy or even find unpleasant, uncomfortable or distasteful.

Begin your search by considering times you were most upset. Let the Talking Tips be your guide.

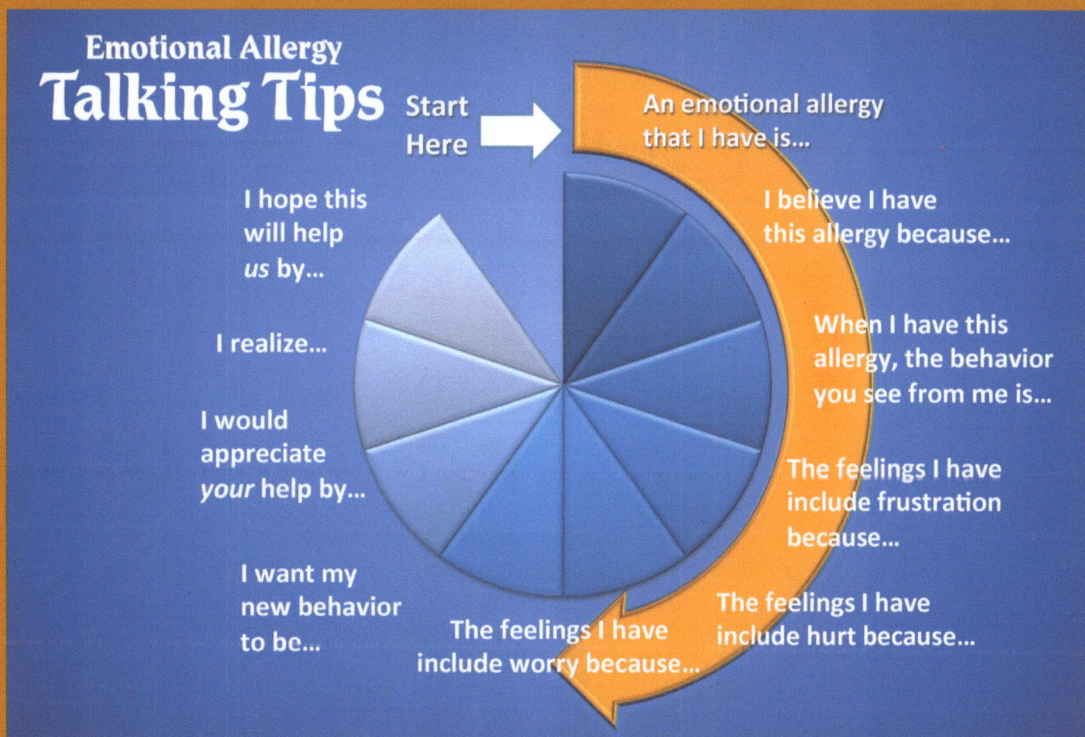

Emotional Allergy
Talking Tips

Start Here →

- An emotional allergy that I have is...
- I believe I have this allergy because...
- When I have this allergy, the behavior you see from me is...
- The feelings I have include frustration because...
- The feelings I have include hurt because...
- The feelings I have include worry because...
- I want my new behavior to be...
- I would appreciate *your* help by...
- I realize...
- I hope this will help *us* by...

PROPHETS 13

GLADIATORS 15

Prophets are well known for the accuracy of their predictions. When it comes to intimacy, they have no trouble making sure their most feared prophesies come true.

By living out, instead of talking through, their hidden beliefs, they will quickly find themselves on loops of increasing distance and despair. Ironically and tragically, that's most likely in the relationships they're most afraid of losing.

The exit ramp from the prophets' loop begins with the courage to face and confide their fears.

Gladiators can appear to be superheroes. But in their closest relationships, unrealistic, perfectionist expectations can lead to disappointment, distance and despair.

High expectations and exemplary performance may hide deeper fears of inadequacy from everyone but the people they most love.

The exit ramp from the gladiators' loop begins with accepting the strengths, challenges, good days, and bad that are a natural part of life. Being good enough and lovable comes from being born.

EMPERORS 16

Emperors, despite all their power and potential, often live in a world of disappointment. No one is likely to meet their expectations for mind-reading.

It's not unusual for emperors and their loved ones to find themselves in a battlefield in which withholding, distance, and angered or pained expressions becomes primary ways of communicating.

The exit ramp from the emperors' loop begins with learning to ask for what they want, not expecting others to read their minds, and generously appreciating loved ones for what they do.

KIDDERS 19

Kidders bring the sandboxes of childhood and adolescent rebellion into nearly every aspect of love relationships long after those stages have passed.

Meaningful hopes for lasting love, intimacy, and happiness can fast become endless competitions in which the relationship, along with everyone counting on it as a stable, secure foundation to life, loses.

The exit ramp from the kidders' loop begins with embracing lasting love and intimacy as an adventure for grown-ups who can find joy in being a pleasure to those they love.

FIBBERS 21

Fibbers are masters of finding what they're looking for, whether it's actually there or not.

Opportunities to discuss and resolve differences that are a natural part of life's passages are lost to hidden agendas, feelings and aspirations that can leave loved ones treating each other like enemies.

The exit ramp from the fibbers' loop begins with becoming comfortable accepting whatever emotions they have, confiding feelings and thoughts with empathy, and recognizing their adult responsibility (and consequences) for their actions.

LONERS 22

Loners decided early on that the world of love and relationships is not a safe place. Fears of loss, betrayal and inadequacy fuel an endless cycle of lost opportunities for stability, happiness, and love.

You can find loners in a constant revolving door of disappointment and despair that sabotages any hopes to fulfill life's big dreams.

The exit ramp from the loners' loop begins with accepting that all relationships end, as life itself ends. What's in our hands is making the most of life and the joys of love and intimacy in the time we have.

PROFESSORS 25

Professors expect themselves to be the masters of everything, even when they're not. That may work in a classroom or office where others depend on good grades and approval. But not in love relationships where empathy and respect matter most.

You can often spot professors through grimaced facial expressions and body language that screams contempt in the face of disagreement or criticism.

The exit ramp from the professors' loop begins with valuing differences in others as a sign of strength, intelligence, respect and maturity.

FIXERS 27

Fixers can be natural helpers, servants and healers, except when they can't. In close relationships, there will be times when we can't fix things for another.

You can find fixers in the environments where they most thrive: making things better for others. When they can't, it can feel devastating for the fixer, whose self-worth may feel deeply wounded, causing distance when what others may most need is empathy and a witness who cares.

The exit ramp from the fixers' loop begins with allowing others to ask for what they want or need.

VILLAINS   28

Villains can feel hopeless and stuck in an unfair world. Afraid to accept responsibility for taking on the challenges of their lives, they measure "love" for others by how they feel about themselves.

You can recognize villains by the revolving door of peaks and valleys they typically experience when it comes to romance. It's not unusual for villains to become cynical about relationships. They don't know their expectations are their own saboteurs.

The exit ramp from the villains' loop begins with accepting themselves as good enough and lovable.

FAKERS   31

Fakers may become so comfortable hiding behind pretentious masks, they forget what's underneath

You can often recognize a faker from the toys they parade - fancy cars, jewels, gifts, money, and more meant to hide them from being truly seen and loved by another person. Fakers can be anyone they think others want them to be, and then resentful of those who get ensnared in their deceitful web.

The exit ramp from the fakers' loop begins with knowing the difference between a package and its contents.

MARTYRS 33

Martyrs are likely to define themselves exclusively through a relationship as a substitute for personal identity. It's not that a martyr is "in a relationship." For martyrs, they are the relationship.

Martyrs can be found clinging by phone, text or in-person to the person they hold completely responsible for their identity and well-being. You will rarely find the martyr happily alone.

The exit ramp from the martyrs' loop begins with embracing the miracle of their lives to be able to truly enjoy the gift of intimacy with others.

SLAYERS 34

Slayers can transform the potential for intimacy into animosity and distance at the speed of light.

You'll frequently find slayers confiding their disappointments to everyone (willing to listen) except their partner. Slayers can be found eagerly soliciting validation and encouraging others to accept the same faulty assumptions and hidden expectations sabotaging their own love life.

The exit ramp from the slayers' loop begins with learning empathy as the foundation of being able to confide their needs and allowing others to also.

If I show you how much I love you and need you in my life, my desire for you might drive you away, so I never show you how much I care. If I don't show you how much you mean to me and how much I care, you feel unloved and you distance from me.
If you are distant from me, you don't love me. Therefore why should I love you?

PROPHETS

Self-fulfilling prophesies are typical for prophets who are so afraid of losing love that they don't show another person how much they matter. For this couple, his decision to act on his fears rather than facing, confiding and working through them left her feeling unloved. That experience triggered her emotional allergy about being in a relationship in which she isn't valued, and fears that she'd be neglected, abandoned or betrayed. Instead of confiding her fears, she reacted by distancing with the belief, "Why should I love you when you don't love me?"

But they do love, want, and need each other. Finding the courage to be vulnerable by confiding their fears to each other offers an opportunity to transform the prophets' loop into deeper experiences of love, intimacy and acceptance.

GLADIATORS

Unrealistic expectations are typical for gladiators who believe they should be competent and successful in every situation. Always.

His fear of accepting and confiding his own humanity had him living a lie. Her emotional allergy was triggered by his increasing distance, which she interpreted as a reflection of her competence, value and importance.

When they fell in love, she cherished knowing that she was a pleasure in his life, as he was in hers. Not long after getting married, neither understood what happened that caused the distance that had become all too familiar.

By confiding in each other, they were able to transform their gladiators' loop into a stronger partnership in which he no longer had to live a lie. She learned to accept that she could help and support him emotionally, while not seeing his fears and bouts of unhappiness as a measure of her self-worth and value to his life.

She was the first to find the courage to confide.

As she spoke, he listened with empathy for how it was for her and repeated back her words to let her know he accurately heard, understood and valued her feelings:

"An emotional allergy that I have is feeling like I can't make you happy when you seem sad and distant from me."

"I believe I have this allergy because I grew up with a dad who was depressed and I saw how much that made my mom suffer and eventually led them to divorce."

"When I have this allergy, the behavior you see from me is anger and distance."

"The feelings I have include frustration because I feel helpless to make you feel better."

"The feelings I have include hurt because I miss our friendship and the fun we used to have."

"The feelings I have include worry or fear because I'm afraid that what happened with my parents' marriage will happen to us too."

"I want my new behavior to be respecting that you have ups and downs that are not about me and asking you what's going on when you seem unhappy or distant."

"I would appreciate your help by honestly telling me what's going on with you so I don't have to guess or assume."

"I realize you've taken on a lot in the last year and that much of it is very difficult, but I know with time and experience you can succeed at anything."

"I hope this will help us by becoming closer and better able to love and support each other through good times and tough ones too."

EMPERORS

When they fell in love they were attracted to each other's confidence, independence and somewhat rebellious nature.

But as a couple, they struggled to cooperate and collaborate in creating the "we" of their life together. The love they felt for each other had turned into animosity and resentment.

Her unrealistic expectations that he could read her mind to know what she wanted and needed led to increasing distance and the feeling that they had become enemies.

His emotional allergy was being triggered by early experiences in which he felt he was never good enough for his demanding mother. He decided to depend only on his own approval and had remained rebellious even though it's not his mother that he married.

This couple's future together depended on her learning to clearly ask for what she wanted and appreciating him for what he did. His part was to realize they're on the same team, and that when he helps her, he's also helping his dreams for their life and happiness together come true.

In class, he confided his emotional allergy:

"An emotional allergy that I have is feeling like no matter what I do, you're never satisfied."

"I believe I have this allergy because of how my mother treated me and dad. It felt like she was always criticizing us with her words and gestures."

"When I have this allergy, the behavior you see from me is I don't do anything and become completely uninterested in want you want or need."

"The feelings I have include frustration because I've tried to help and it's never seemed good enough."

"The feelings I have include hurt because I thought when I got out of my parents' house I'd never have to go through being treated this way again."

"The feelings I have include worry or fear because I feel like we're becoming my mother and father, which was not a happy relationship."

"I want my new behavior to be asking you to let me know what you want or need from me, and doing my best to help out without feeling resentful."

"I would appreciate your help by asking me to do what you want instead of expecting me to know, and also showing me appreciation for what I do."

"I realize we can work this out if we both want to and that you're not my mother."

"I hope this will help us by not arguing or feeling like we have to avoid each other and giving ourselves a chance to enjoy our life together."

If you tell me what you want, I won't do it because I resent feeling controlled. If you don't tell me what you want, then I may try to figure it out. What do you want? I'll never know.
If I do what you want, and it's not what I want to do, I resent it. I believe you would resent it if I do what I want to do, as it's not what you want to do. So I never do what I want. I'm miserable. I hate you for making me miserable.

KIDDERS

Like emperors, kidders can easily got stuck in a bitter loop. As children, this couple had more than their share of sandbox fights. But they're not kids anymore, and their bedroom is not a childhood sandbox.

His emotional allergy comes from being ordered around. He developed resentment to being told what to do during times when he had to follow orders. Although she had nothing to do with those experiences and period of his life, she's paying the price.

Instead of talking it through, she's reacting. If he won't listen to her, she not interested in what he wants. They're both miserable.

For these kidders, ending the cycle of bitterness and transforming their loop means he'll need to confide what it felt like to have to follow orders for so long and realize if he keeps "handing her the bill" for those experiences, their relationship will pay the price. Her willingness to listen with empathy and embrace the gift of being a pleasure to each other will give them the fresh start they both desperately want.

My commitment to you is too restrictive for me. I wish to change it. I cannot tell you. You would be upset. To see you is to experience my guilt. I will find reasons to be angry with you, so I need not feel guilty. I will provoke you, anger you, drive you away, to give me a reason to be angry with you... so I can feel justified in my behavior, in breaking my commitment. And not feel guilty.
If I tell you how I feel, you will be angry. You will attack me or withhold from me. I am afraid of your anger and your distance. I can't tell you. I live a lie.

FIBBERS

Fibbers will find what they're looking for whether it's there or not. Her fear of confiding feelings that could upset her husband was sabotaging any hope for their marriage. Instead, she was finding reasons to provoke him.

He was angry. But instead of letting her know, he held it in, living a lie, and paying a heavy price emotionally and physically.

When she finally mustered the courage to confide, the couple became closer as they understood each other and were able to work through their differences.

Her confiding began with sharing her allergy.

"An emotional allergy that I have is feeling like I'm completely dependent on you and don't have the freedom to pursue interests independently."

"I believe I have this allergy because I saw my mom spend my entire childhood being a devoted homemaker, wife and mother, only to have dad eventually walk out on her."

"When I have this allergy, the behavior you see from me is picking on you and blaming you so I don't feel guilty about wanting more."

"The feelings I have include frustration because I hate how I feel when I upset you and also how I feel when I hide my feelings."

"The feelings I have include hurt because there's so much anger between us and I haven't known how to make things better."

"The feelings I have include worry or fear because I'm afraid that you'll leave me if I tell you what I want and that I'll be unhappy forever if I don't tell you and don't do what I want."

"I want my new behavior to be letting you know that I love you, am committed to you, our marriage and family, but that I also have a need to pursue interests outside our home and relationship."

"I would appreciate your help by supporting my desire to finish my degree and have a career that's fulfilling and rewarding."

"I realize you and the kids depend on me for many things and that we'll need to figure out how to balance that with the time I put into school and, hopefully, my career."

"I hope this will help us by knowing we both want the best for each other and our family. I also hope this will help us stop arguing and instead talk about things when they come up so we can rebuild the amazing relationship we both want to last for the rest of our lives."

LONERS

Loners experience love and intimacy as a revolving door of disappointment, despair and constant, short-lived new beginnings.

This couple became cynical about the potential for lasting love long before they met. As long as neither were willing to risk confiding their fears, they became increasingly distant and nearly lost each other.

They finally realized what they were doing to each other when she recognized after a PAIRS exercise the early decisions she'd made about love and relationships, and how unfair it was that she was blaming him.

He realized that while she appreciated the things he did for her, it was him and their life together she valued most.

With time and skill, they created a new cycle in which each was willing to confide their fears instead of pushing each other away. In place of joyless, loveless early decisions, empathy and compassion became building blocks to creating the happiness they both wanted.

She began by sharing her emotional allergy:

"An emotional allergy that I have is needing you or anyone else."

"I believe I have this allergy because of all the people I lost in my life, I decided I couldn't count on anyone except myself."

"When I have this allergy, the behavior you see from me is looking for evidence that you're going to leave me too."

"The feelings I have include frustration because I'm tired of always starting over."

"The feelings I have include hurt because everyone I've counted on has died or left me."

"The feelings I have include worry or fear because I'm afraid that's how my life will always be."

"I want my new behavior to be letting you know when I get scared instead of pushing you away."

"I would appreciate your help by just hearing me and holding me during those times, and reassuring me of your commitment when I'm afraid."

"I realize you choose me as your partner for life, love me, accept me, and haven't done anything to deserve the way I've been treating you."

"I hope this will help us by helping me confront my fears, become better able to accept your love, and show you the love and gratitude I feel for you."

If we don't agree, one of us must be wrong. If it is me, that means I am bad, stupid, ignorant, or inadequate. So it can't be me. I must prove that it is you, so I won't feel like a failure.
If you criticize me, I feel inadequate. If you compliment me, you are placating or controlling me by saying only what you think I want to hear.

PROFESSORS

Professors are so afraid of not appearing to know all the answers that they aren't able to live in the world of intimacy where differences are a natural part of close relationships.

When he was willing to confide how beat up he felt when he made a mistake growing up in a family of competitive siblings and the decisions he made to protect himself by always insisting he was right, she discovered even stronger feelings of love and compassion for her husband. Her empathy helped him realize he didn't have to pretend to know it all and that he could admit he had much to learn. He stopped being super critical of those who had different thoughts, feelings or perspective from his own.

As he stopped criticizing her, she became better able to accept the sincerity of his compliments. Deeper levels of trust and acceptance became a new foundation for the happy, fulfilling marriage they're building together.

If I tell you how I feel, you will interrupt, correct, give advice, judge, or dismiss my feelings. I feel betrayed, angry, frustrated. I won't tell you my feelings. I distance.
If I were what I should be, you would be happy. I would be able to solve (fix) everything. Since I can't, your unhappiness makes me feel inadequate, guilty, angry - at you. I distance myself from you.

FIXERS

Fixers are so busy inflicting advice they often miss the opportunity to give what's wanted most: a partner who can be a caring witness to our lives and a good listener.

When they were dating, she liked knowing he "had it handled," no matter what the challenge required. But that changed in the early years of their marriage. As she took on helping her mother get through cancer treatment and increasing frustration at work, she came home wanting him to hear and comfort her, knowing she was dealing with issues that weren't in his hands to fix.

But at the times she needed him most, he became more and more distant and showed anger towards her she couldn't understand.

When she finally was able to confront his habit of interrupting or dismissing her altogether, his first response was even more anger and distance. By the next day, however, he was ready to confide what he realized.

"An emotional allergy that I have is feeling like I can't make things better for someone I love."

"I believe I have this allergy because during the months my dad was sick, I felt completely helpless and lost. It was like my whole world was collaps-

ing and I couldn't do anything about it."

"When I have this allergy, the behavior you see from me is quickly trying to make things better and finding an excuse to blame you or withdraw from you when I can't."

"The feelings I have include frustration because I couldn't help my dad when he needed me and, although I know it's not the same, I feel like I can't help you when you need me."

"The feelings I have include hurt because I feel helpless and worthless when I can't fix a problem for someone I love."

"The feelings I have include worry or fear because I'm afraid if I can't make things better for you when you're upset, you won't need me."

"I want my new behavior to be letting you vent without interrupting, and asking you if you want my help or advice before giving it."

"I would appreciate your help by telling me when you just want to vent and that what you want is for me to just listen and not give advice."

"I realize I've been blaming you and making things worse. I'm sorry for that."

"I hope this will help our relationship by making it safe for you to confide in me and know that I want to always be there for you."

VILLAINS

For the villain, life is no picnic. They live in a world of unfulfilled expectations, broken promises, disappointment, abandon and despair.

In college, he thought he had it all with her by his side. He felt loved, valued, envied and popular. She enjoyed being his girlfriend. They didn't talk much, but she felt safe knowing he was there.

After college, he struggled. He couldn't find a job, relied on his parents for help, and no longer felt like the popular guy he'd been on campus.

In the face of her fears for their future, she began withdrawing. She stayed busy with her job, family and girlfriends, trying to be around him as little as possible. The last thing she wanted was for him to know she was frightened and didn't know how to help him through his slump.

As his anger became routine, there were several times when they both thought the relationship was over until the night she courageously took his hands in hers and confided her fears.

Those moments were the wake up call he needed. He responded to her fears with empathy. The blaming stopped, as did the distance.

A few weeks later, he found a job; not the perfect job he'd been hoping for, but a job where he earned a living and a chance to prove himself.

Most important, they knew they could count on each other and the future they were creating.

Her courage to confide, and his empathetic response, changed the course of their life.

"An emotional allergy that I have is feeling like if I let you know when I'm scared, you'll decide I'm not competent, don't know what to do, and won't respect me."

"I believe I have this allergy because of growing up in a home where no matter how bad things were, we always had to smile and act like everything was wonderful."

"When I have this allergy, the behavior you see from me is staying away from you."

"The feelings I have include frustration because I don't know how to help you and don't like acting like everything's okay when it isn't."

"The feelings I have include hurt because I feel sad when I see you upset and I can't do anything to help."

"The feelings I have include worry or fear because I'm afraid when you realize I can't make you happy, you'll find someone else who does."

"I want my new behavior to be accepting that I can't be responsible for your happiness, but I can still love you and be there to cheer for you and listen to you."

"I would appreciate your help by doing what you need to do to get out of your slump and not giving me looks and saying things that feel like you think it's my fault."

"I realize it's a difficult time for us and a lot of other people. That doesn't mean anything is wrong. We just need to be patient and keeping working at it."

"I hope this will help us by getting to a place where we can be close again, not feeling like we have to hide from or blame each other, and being there to support and love one another the ways we can."

If you were what you should be, I would be happy, successful, popular, attractive, virile, potent, sexy. I am not. It's your fault.
If I let you get close to me, you will find out my secrets, my fears, how inadequate I really am. You won't love (respect) me. I must keep you at a distance.

If you say you love me, you either don't know me, want to use me, or are stupid and have poor judgment. I can't love you.
If I am what you want me to be, I dislike myself. I resent you wanting me to be what I don't like. If I am myself, you won't like me. I resent you for not letting me be myself.

FAKERS

Fakers can be a plastic surgeon's dream come true. And also realtors, decorators, fancy car dealerships, jewelry stores, and exclusive boutiques.

With all her natural beauty, he was always looking for something more. Fuller lips, perkier breasts, bigger rear … it was endless. For years, she went through it all, wanting to be exactly what he wanted from her, until the afternoon she discovered that after all she'd gone through, he was flirting (and maybe more) with an attractive young woman at his office.

After nearly a dozen painful elective procedures over three years, she'd had enough. It didn't matter any more that he was paying for it. Even before she began to suspect his cheating, she resented him for always trying to change her.

When she declared, "Enough!" he felt betrayed. He'd long believed it was his generosity she valued. If she wasn't going to accept that, he couldn't imagine a future together.

Although she confided her feelings to him, and the emotional allergy being triggered, instead of listening with empathy as she became vulnerable, he argued, disagreed, and said he considered her new found independence to be a deal-breaker.

Three weeks after moving out, she discovered the woman from his office was spending nights at the home they'd recently shared. She couldn't help but feel a sense of justice when that woman left him and his office a few months later when she began dating a younger man.

Her experience helped her learn what didn't fit for her when it came to love and intimacy. As she became loving and accepting of herself, she was able to enjoy others who did too.

If you need me, I feel obligated, pressured, burdened. If you don't need me, I believe you don't care.
If you don't love me, stay with me, I will die. Therefore, I must cling to you no matter what the price. The more I cling, the more you feel smothered and distance from me. The more you withdraw, the more I cling.

MARTYRS

Martyrs experience themselves as fully dependent on others for their survival, believing their identity, self-worth, and existence doesn't exist separate from another person. For the martyr, there's only "we."

Throughout high school, she liked knowing that he needed her. His life was hers. When not in the few classes they didn't take together, they spent practically every waking minute with each other. When they had to be apart, it was rare that more than a few minutes passed before they were talking on the phone or texting. If she didn't answer or respond within moments, he'd become panicked and sad, which would quickly become a heated topic of discussion when they finally connected.

He was thrilled when she became pregnant in the spring of their senior year. His fear that she'd leave him faded with the belief that their child would keep them together forever.

When her mother took her to doctor appointments without him, he felt enraged. When she didn't feel well as the pregnancy progressed and needed restful time apart, his sadness verged on melancholy.

One week after a stressful graduation, she miscarried. She waited a week before telling him.

When she did, he showed little empathy for the pain and sadness she was going through.

Afterwards, she found herself wanting less and less to do with him, spending more time with girlfriends she'd neglected since they'd started dating. His calls, texts and uninvited visits to her home became increasingly annoying. The more desperately he reached out, the more she wanted to run away from him for good.

By late summer, she decided to go to college across the country. She told him just days before leaving, along with the news that she wanted a break from their relationship. As he anxiously began sharing plans to move away with her, she became angry. Her decision was final, she said. As he tried every which way to convince her that he needed her and couldn't survive without her, her sympathy transformed into resentment. She didn't want to see or hear from him anymore.

By the end of her first year in college, she was in a relationship with someone she valued for his sense of independence. She liked that she was often the one reaching out for time together instead of him. She valued knowing they could be there for each other, but also enjoy time apart without anger, fear or anxiety.

She didn't see her former boyfriend when she came home for the summer, although she heard he too was in another relationship. She felt grateful for the good times they'd had, but even more so for the lessons she'd learned.

SLAYERS

She was miserable, and he was too. More than a few times, she hesitated to open wedding gifts, wondering if they didn't get through six months, should she give the presents back?

The animosity came out in full force during what was supposed to be their perfect honeymoon. He'd saved up for months, made all the plans, and surprised her with the trip to Italy he thought she'd always wanted to take.

What he didn't know is that she didn't want to go to Italy generally. She wanted to go to Rome. Instead of telling him, she stewed and brewed. There wasn't a happy moment between them during their week in Milan. He had no idea what had happened between their wedding and what he thought would be the gift of a lifetime. On the overnight flight home, they barely exchanged a word.

The pictures from their trip told the story better than they could. Amidst the beauty and romance of Milan, he was always smiling as she frowned or looked away in every shot.

Her girlfriends validated how resentful she felt that he had made plans for their honeymoon without involving her. They couldn't believe she'd been to Italy without going to Rome. They didn't blame her for being angry. Only one friend asked, "So what did he say when you told him you wanted to go to Rome?" Somewhat dumbfounded, she admitted she hadn't. After a dinner of leftovers that night, she asked him to listen as she confided why she was so upset.

"An emotional allergy that I have is feeling like if you love me, you would know what I want without me having to tell you. When you don't, I feel like you don't care about me and I become withholding."

"I believe I have this allergy because of growing up in a home where my parents and others always knew what I wanted and did it for me without me having to ask. I had the idea you weren't supposed to ask."

"When I have this allergy, the behavior you see from me is anger and distance towards you when you don't give me what I want or expect."

"The feelings I have include frustration because instead of just having an amazing trip together, I was angry the whole time of our honeymoon because we went to Milan and not Rome."

"The feelings I have include hurt because I realize I've been so mean to you when you were doing something you thought would be what I wanted."

"The feelings I have include worry or fear because I'm afraid you won't forgive me for ruining our honeymoon and that we might not get over this."

"I want my new behavior to be letting you know what I want if something is important to me instead of expecting you to know."

"I would appreciate your help by asking me what I think before making major plans or decisions for us."

"I realize you spent so much money on a trip you didn't really want to take because you thought I did."

"I hope this will help us by learning that we need to talk about big decisions that involve both of us and that I can, and will, appreciate what you do even if it's not always exactly what I want."

35

Seth Eisenberg, left, at graduation of PAIRS class for wounded warriors.

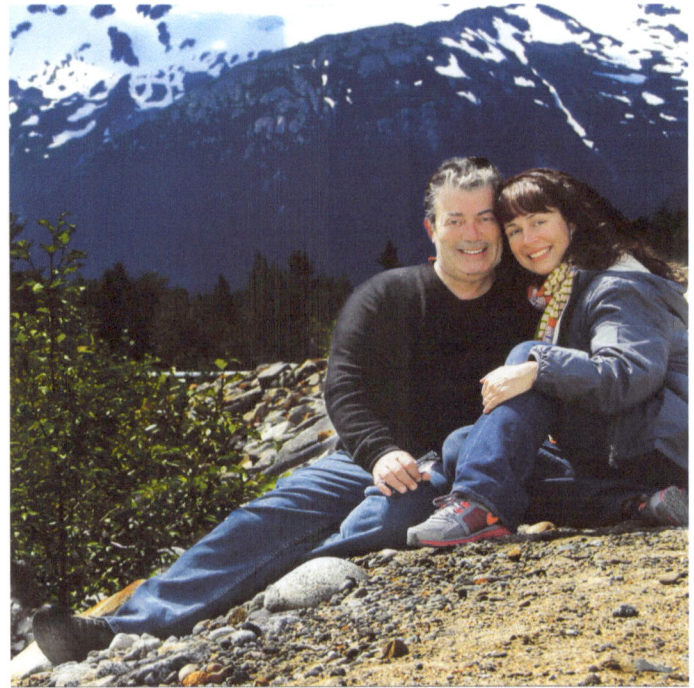

Seth and Stephanie Eisenberg at the Alaska/Canadian border.

ABOUT THE AUTHOR

SETH DANIEL EISENBERG is CEO of the nonprofit PAIRS Foundation in Miami, Florida, an industry leader in marriage and relationship education since 1983. His work bridging evidence-based skills training and technology has touched the lives of hundreds of thousands of adults and youngsters.

The youngest by seven years of four siblings, Seth grew up with a working single mother after she and his father divorced during his early childhood. From the time he can remember, he silently pledged that he would never do what his parents had done when he grew up. Yet during the childhood of his first two sons, his first marriage ended. With the painful realization that good intentions were not enough for him and others raised in the shadows of divorce, Seth became a passionate advocate for relationship skills training that was practical, proven and could be widely accessible.

PAIRS, which stands for "Practical Application of Intimate Relationship Skills," has been prominently featured in the national media and recognized as a Best Practice by the VA, Planetree and others. Classes are offered worldwide by PAIRS trained professionals.

www.ingramcontent.com/pod-product-compliance
Lightning Source LLC
Chambersburg PA
CBHW061100090426
42742CB00003B/101